CONQUERING NEGATIVE BODY IMAGE

CONQUERING NEGATIVE BODY IMAGE

VIOLA JONES AND EDWARD WILLETT

ROSEN
PUBLISHING®

New York

Published in 2016 by The Rosen Publishing Group, Inc.
29 East 21st Street, New York, NY 10010

First Edition

Library of Congress Cataloging in Publication Data

Jones, Viola.
 Conquering negative body image / Viola Jones and Edward Willett. — First edition.
     pages cm. — (Conquering eating disorders)
 Audience: Grades 7–12.
 Includes bibliographical references and index.
 ISBN 978-1-4994-6205-0 (library bound)
 1. Body image in adolescence—Juvenile literature. 2. Body image—Social aspects—United States—Juvenile literature. 3. Self-acceptance in adolescence—Juvenile literature. I. Willett, Edward, 1959– II. Title.
 RA777.25.J66 2016
 616.85'2600835—dc23
                                2015019516

For many of the images in this book, the people photographed are models. The depictions do not imply actual situations or events.

Manufactured in the United States of America

CONTENTS

What Do You See When You Look in the Mirror?

CHAPTER ONE

Think about your relationship with your body. Do you appreciate it for all the things it does? It is a complex system that allows you to run, jump, lift, stretch, and even learn new things in school. But you might not consider all the functions your body performs because you are focusing on how it appears when you look at yourself in the mirror. You might compare yourself to someone at school or your favorite movie star and assume that the person has a better life than you because he or she is thinner and more attractive.

This is what's known as a negative body image, and it can get in the way of developing into a happy, healthy human being. In today's society, body image is more than just the mental picture you have of what your body looks like. For many, body image is also a reflection of how they feel about themselves and their lives. People with a negative body image believe that if they don't look right, other things, such as their personality, intelligence, social skills, or capabilities, also aren't right. They think that if they fix their bodies, all of their other problems will disappear. This can result in unhealthy weight management

When you look in the mirror, do you like what you see, or are you unhappy with your reflection? Our perception of our own bodies can be accurate or drastically distorted.

practices and an unhealthy relationship with food. People excessively diet and exercise out of fear of gaining weight.

Where Does Your Body Image Come From?

Your body image is influenced by many different things. It is influenced by family, friends, and a culture that is obsessed with weight, body shape, dieting, and food. All people have negative thoughts and feelings about their body at some point in their life. But when it becomes more than a passing concern, when people base their happiness and self-worth on what they eat, how often they exercise, and how much they weigh, they are suffering from a negative body image. This outlook causes people to believe that all their experiences in life are affected by their appearance and body weight.

Even worse, when this preoccupation with food and weight turns into an obsession, it can result in a full-blown eating disorder. According to the National Eating Disorders Association (NEDA), more than eleven million people in the United States are suffering from an eating disorder such as bulimia nervosa or anorexia nervosa, and another twenty-five million are battling binge eating disorder.

The problems surrounding body image can be especially difficult for teens. Adolescence is a time when you might feel confused about the changes happening to your body. These changes are a natural part of growing up, but they can make you feel out of control and unhappy with your appearance. As a result, you might turn to unhealthy eating habits, which can lead to an eating disorder. This can seriously damage your physical and emotional health.

Nobody is born with a negative body image. It is something that you learn, something that develops over time. As you grow older, your experiences are shaped by the different messages you get from society. And those messages often connect personal success and happiness with being thin and beautiful. If people feel they don't measure up to those ideals of success, then they tend to disregard any other real accomplishments. Having a negative body image can seriously distort the way you look at yourself and your life.

Having a negative body image can be very dangerous if it's not addressed. The good news is, because a negative body image is something you learn, it also can be unlearned. Do you know how to recognize a negative body image, what the causes and consequences are, and how to overcome a negative body image? If you work on learning to love and respect your body right now, you'll have the time, energy, and willpower to focus on the most important part of your being—who you are inside.

Cultural Beauty Ideals

People throughout the world have very specific—and very different—ideas of what makes someone beautiful. This idea is often referred to as the beauty ideal because it represents what is thought of as "perfect." But in many cases, the beauty ideal is impossible and unhealthy for most people to achieve. In the United States, this ideal is constantly promoted through messages and images from the media (advertising, fashion magazines, television, movies, and videos). When people don't see themselves in these images, they believe there is something wrong with them. If they constantly judge themselves against this ideal, they will always feel that they're not good enough.

The beauty ideal is always changing. In the 1950s and 1960s, Marilyn Monroe was America's most celebrated sex symbol. But by today's standards, she might be considered overweight and out of shape. Today, the ideal is an impossibly thin, waiflike model who looks nothing like the majority of Americans. But since we are bombarded by these images, people think it's the norm, or standard, for everybody. Ultimately, no matter what the current trend is, the beauty ideal has nothing to do with reality. In reality, people come in a variety of shapes and sizes, which are determined mainly by their genetic makeup.

The beauty ideal changes, depending on the society. In the 1950s and 1960s, actress Marilyn Monroe was the American ideal, but her look is not necessarily in fashion today.

Nonetheless, advertisers in the beauty and fashion industries make it seem that if you don't strive for the beauty ideal, you won't be successful or happy in life. Advertising relies on and targets this feeling of inadequacy to sell products that will supposedly improve your appearance. Advertisers want you to believe the beauty ideal is a goal we can achieve so that we will spend money on products such as fat-free foods, diet drinks, weight-loss pills, skin products, makeup, exercise videos and equipment, and fashion magazines.

Both Males and Females Can Be Affected

Anyone can suffer from a negative body image. In our society, girls feel more pressure to look good and reach a beauty ideal. At a young age, females are taught to believe that physical appearance is more important than anything else. They believe their physical appearance defines their identity.

In fact, one study conducted by the American Association of University Women found that middle-school girls reported that their looks were the most important factor in feeling good about themselves. And almost half of them are unhappy with the way their bodies look. Girls start voicing dissatisfaction with their weight or body shape by the age of six, according to the Centers for Disease Control and the National Eating Disorders Association. By elementary school age, the study found, girls fear looking fat more than they fear losing their parents, getting cancer, or experiencing nuclear war. Generally, boys are not as vulnerable as girls to negative body image. This is because boys are taught by society and their families to define themselves more by abilities than appearance. Boys are encouraged more than girls to express themselves and be aggressive to achieve what they want. But boys, too, can be

Young girls are taught that they should look like runway models if they want to be happy and successful in life. The truth is, looking like a model doesn't guarantee happiness.

affected by a negative body image. When they don't measure up to an ideal body that is very lean and muscular, they—like girls—might hurt their bodies by overeating or not eating at all. According to a 2012 study published in *Pediatrics*, 40 percent of 2,793 middle and high school boys surveyed viewed the ideal body as toned and muscular. In the hopes of achieving that body, two-thirds of this group changed their diets, exercised, and used protein powders and steroids to bulk up and achieve a more muscular appearance.

It's not just girls who are bombarded with images of bodies that are nearly impossible to attain. Boys feel the pressure to measure up to models and actors they see in magazines and in movies.

Experts agree there is a clear connection between negative body image and eating disorders. And because females are more vulnerable to negative body image, they are also more likely than males to suffer from an eating disorder. According to the National Eating Disorders Association, twenty million women suffer from an eating disorder in their lifetime. And the number of males who have eating disorders has increased to ten million. No one is immune to these problems. And, according to research conducted at the

School of Public Health, University of Minneapolis, and published in August 2006, teens who have negative feelings about their bodies are more apt to binge eat, smoke, eat unbalanced meals, and exercise less than those who possess positive body images.

How Do I Know if I Have a Negative Body Image?

It's important to recognize the signs of a negative body image. Once you recognize the problem, you can work on accepting your body. The sooner you address the problem, the more likely you are to overcome it.

• Do you constantly look at yourself in the mirror?
• Are you afraid of getting fat?
• Do you think about food a lot?
• Do you constantly compare your body with those of others?
• Do you say negative things about your body to other people?
• Do you say mean things about your body to yourself?
• Do you get mad at yourself or your body after looking at magazines or watching television?
• Do you avoid social activities because you think others will find you unattractive?
• Do you avoid eating around other people?
• Do you wish you could change the way you look?

If you answered yes to most of these questions, a negative body image might be affecting your life and you should consider getting help. Without help, you might be putting yourself at risk for an eating disorder.

Many of these "signs" are perfectly common thoughts to have as you develop from a child to a teen to an adult. Everyone is unhappy with the way they look from time to time. In addition, many of us strive to be a little thinner or more muscular. But the difference between the occasional wish and constant feelings of inadequacy, bordering on obsession, is significant. Take one day and write down every thought you have about your body. Then review your notes. Do they indicate that you might have a negative body image?

CHAPTER TWO

What Contributes to a Negative Body Image?

Even though kids are criticizing their bodies at increasingly younger ages, there is a time when we are blissfully unaware that we might not meet the ideal standards of beauty. Do you remember being a little kid, when all you cared about was running and playing? You ate when you were hungry and stopped when you were full.

When did it all change? When do we start to think constantly about how we look to other people? And what makes us do it? There are many different factors that can affect our self-image.

Adolescence: A Time of Change

Puberty, a developmental stage that occurs between the ages of nine and sixteen, is a time when young bodies become adult bodies. As you enter puberty, your body goes through a number of changes. You might feel out of control because your body seems to be doing things you've never felt before—some of which are uncomfortable or embarrassing.

Females naturally gain weight during puberty. This is the body's way of preparing for menstruation and childbirth. Hips start to widen, breasts begin to develop, and body fat increases. It's all part of the process of becoming a healthy woman. But these physical changes can sometimes trigger a negative body image because of all the images of very thin women and advertisements for diets and weight loss products that surround Americans. For males, too, puberty can be a troubling time if their bodies don't achieve a very lean and muscular ideal. As a result, young people who dislike their bodies might begin to diet.

Adolescence is one of the most stressful times of life, when you deal with countless physical changes as well as social pressures.

The changes that occur during puberty affect both our minds and our bodies. Witnessing physical changes that you have no control over can lead to the development of negative feelings.

It's a time when fitting into a group can feel very important. Teens always know what is "in" and "out," and it seems important to adhere to the societal ideal. You might even think that if you reach the ideal, you'll be accepted and liked by everyone.

However, just when it seems important to fit in, it is also the most dangerous time to diet. Adolescent bodies are growing and developing into healthy adult bodies—and they can't do it without proper nutrition.

Low Self-Confidence

Another factor that might lead to a negative body image is low self-esteem. Self-esteem is the way you feel about yourself and your abilities. People with high self-esteem have confidence in their capabilities, and they like themselves the way they are. Those with low self-esteem have serious doubts about what they can achieve and often feel too scared to try new things because they fear they will not succeed.

Self-esteem is very difficult to measure, and it's also hard to figure out exactly where it comes from, but one thing is sure: self-esteem is closely related to body image. Research has shown that females suffer from low self-esteem because they think they are not desirable or beautiful. This means they believe their self-worth is dependent upon how others view their bodies and their looks.

Research also shows that before age ten, girls are more emotionally and physically confident than boys. But as they hit the teen years, something starts to change. Females start to lose their self-confidence at the same time their bodies begin to change. This connection results in an intense focus on their bodies. When they don't receive acceptance from others about how they look, they suffer from low self-esteem and begin to question their self-worth.

Adolescents who are not comfortable in their bodies and feel that they don't fit in can develop problems with confidence. For girls in particular, self-confidence suffers during puberty.

Social Pressure

During adolescence, your friends can have a tremendous influence on what you think and do. Peers become very important as you struggle to find your own identity. As you become more independent from your parents, your friends are the ones you go to for approval and acceptance.

But your peers can put a lot of pressure on you to conform to society's standards. And much of the time this pressure can be mean and cruel. It might even seem as if hating your own body is the hip thing to do. Girls often engage in "fat talk," complaining about their bodies, always finding fault with them. As Mary Pipher wrote in her bestselling book *Reviving Ophelia: Saving the Selves of Adolescent Girls* (1995), "Girls punish other girls for failing to achieve the same impossible goals that they are failing to achieve." If all your friends talk about how fat and ugly they think they are, you may begin to feel the same.

During the teen years, peer groups become more influential than family units. It might feel more important to look and act exactly like your friends rather than being an individual.

Unfortunately, this kind of talk feeds off itself, becoming an unhealthy cycle that is difficult to break. Even worse, your friends can encourage you to engage in unhealthy behaviors. Many females learn about eating disorders from their friends and compete to be the thinnest or the smallest. According to some experts, teenagers are particularly susceptible to peer pressure, which might help to explain why the highest rates of some eating disorders, such as anorexia nervosa, happen during the teen years. However, most medical professionals agree that social pressure by itself probably does not cause an eating disorder. There are usually other factors involved, including biological, mental, or emotional aspects.

Your Family

Your family influences how you feel about food and your body. Parents tell you what and how much you should eat. Even though you learn that candy and sweets are unhealthy, you receive such foods as rewards for good behavior. These mixed messages about food can create some complex eating problems.

Family behaviors around eating habits can have an impact on body image, especially for females. If you see your mother always worrying about her weight, going on and off diets, it sends a powerful message and might make everybody in the family believe that worrying about weight is normal and expected.

Families also can cause negative body image if parents have unreasonably high expectations for their children. These expectations can make you feel inadequate, depressed, or guilty when they don't match your interests. You might take your frustrations out on your body through dieting or excessive exercise as a way to assert control.

We develop our first feelings about food and our bodies from our family. When parents emphasize the importance of healthy habits from the start, their children are more likely to develop healthier attitudes toward eating.

The Media's Influence

You see them everywhere—perfect, beautiful women and men with toned bodies, flawless skin, voluminous hair, and straight gleaming teeth. Anywhere you look—magazines, television, movies, even video games—you can't get away from seeing females and males who either look like or actually are fashion models, staring you down and making you feel less than perfect.

But the truth is, these "perfect" models look this way for many reasons. First, they are usually wearing heavy makeup (even to achieve the "natural" look)—so much that you probably wouldn't even recognize models if you saw them on the street without their makeup. Special camera angles and lighting add to the illusion of perfection.

Most pictures of women in fashion magazines are airbrushed or altered by a computer. This means that after the photo is taken, professionals use special tools to correct any imperfections that show up in the photo and might make the model look less than ideal (or more like a typical human being). Another important fact to remember about women and men you see in the media is that many of them have had plastic surgery. In addition, some may actually be starving themselves in order to stay thin. As Academy Award-winning actress Julianne Moore told Shape.com, "I hate dieting. I hate having to do it to be the 'right' size. I'm hungry all the time. I think I'm a slender person, but the industry apparently doesn't. All actresses are hungry all the time, I think."

A study published on March 22, 2000, in the *Journal of the American Medical Association* (*JAMA*) found that in the previous thirty years, the average BMI (body mass index, a number that is calculated by using a person's weight in kilograms divided by the square of that person's height in meters) of Miss America Pageant contestants had dropped by one-third. By 1990, it was down to 18, well

There is no doubt that celebrities are extremely good-looking people. However, in person, without the layers of makeup, the wardrobe, and the airbrushing, you can see that they might not always meet the beauty ideal they've helped create.

below the World Health Organization's (WHO) criteria for malnutrition. Some pageant contestants might starve themselves to achieve such skinny bodies. They might work out an average of fourteen hours per week. Some might work out thirty-five hours each week.

Society is filled with images of perfection because the beauty ideal sells. Advertisers promote the beauty ideal as if it were the real thing because they believe you will spend and spend to try to reach the ideal. Think about all the things you can buy that promise to make you thinner or have better skin, softer hair, whiter teeth, or bigger muscles. The beauty industry wants you to buy perfume, low-fat foods, exercise equipment, cosmetics, and clothes. Fashion magazines push the beauty ideal the hardest because they want to sell magazines as well as the products advertised inside.

The beauty industry is harmful because it tricks people into spending money on products that won't really help them meet the beauty ideal because it is a physical impossibility. And it's almost impossible to escape the beauty industry's messages. They are everywhere. Accepting them and believing in them can severely damage your feelings about your body and yourself. According to a research study on social issues, today's media ideal of thinness for females is achievable by less than 5 percent of the female population.

A clear-cut example of the power of images from Hollywood and Madison Avenue comes from the island of Fiji, where eating great quantities has always been an important part of the culture and where the ideal beauty has a robust, fleshy figure. The introduction of television to Fiji in the 1990s had a significant impact on that society's beauty ideal. According to the Harvard Eating Disorders Center, teenage girls on Fiji who watched TV at least three nights per week were 50 percent more likely than others to see themselves as too fat, and 30 percent more likely to diet, even though they weren't overweight.

Sexual Abuse

Some research has shown that a negative body image can be caused by sexual abuse. When sexual abuse occurs, especially at a young age, the victim might experience a great deal of discomfort with his or her body. The body serves as a reminder of the horrible experience, and he or she might feel responsible for the abuse. As a consequence, victims of sexual abuse might think of their bodies as objects to be despised and punished.

Another way sexual abuse might play a part in causing a negative body image is that girls who are sexually abused at a young age might be afraid of entering puberty and becoming women. Victims might worry that looking more like a woman will bring more abuse. So these girls might starve themselves in hopes of stopping the development of their bodies and menstrual periods, which are a natural part of womanhood. Victims might believe that if they stay thin, their abuser will leave them alone.

Sexual abuse is a serious crime. If you feel you have been sexually abused, it is essential that you find a trusted adult you can talk to privately about your experiences. Instead of punishing yourself, try to take steps to get the help you need and deserve.

People who suffer from negative body image might have one of these contributing factors, or they might have a combination of several. Negative body image is a very complex issue. Ultimately, there is no single cause or single cure. No matter how it developed, you will need to address the contributing issues before you can overcome having a negative body image. It's essential to get to the root of the problem before it gets too big.

MYTHS and *FACTS*

MYTH Other people will like me if I'm pretty and thin.

Looks are not a key to happiness. Your friends like you for who you are. People respond to self-confidence and happiness, not vanity.

MYTH Fat is bad.

The internal weight regulatory system limits just how much long-term control we have over our weight. At certain points in our lives—such as puberty—young people naturally add more body fat. In addition, there are genetic factors beyond your control that determine your appearance. Humans come in a vast variety of body shapes and sizes—including yours!

MYTH Thin is good.

Although obesity does pose some health risks, it's not correct to say that thin people are healthier than overweight people. Thin people may have gotten that way by eating an inadequate diet or smoking heavily or abusing drugs.

MYTH Dieting is an effective way to lose weight.

When you're hungry, your metabolism slows down and your body tends to hang on to more of the calories you take in. Ninety percent of weight lost through dieting is regained—usually with additional pounds.

MYTHS and *FACTS*

MYTH It's too much work to make healthy food choices.

Eat a balanced variety of wholesome food and enjoy the occasional treat. Spend enough time engaged in physical activity to stay fit. Look for realistic role models who will make you feel good about yourself. None of these things are hard if you make them a regular part of your life.

MYTH As long as I eat sensibly and am committed to exercise, I can become thin and keep my thin body image stable.

People come in every shape and size. Being thin is not just a result of diet, exercise, and commitment. It is also a matter of genetics, and whether you have inherited thinness.

CHAPTER THREE

The Dangers of Having a Negative Body Image

So what's the big deal if you wish you were thinner or more muscular? You're not hurting anyone, right? Actually, having a negative body image can lead to many other mental and physical health risks. If gone unchecked, many of these problems can stay with you for life.

Unhealthy Dieting

When people feel unhappy with their bodies, they usually feel a diet is the answer to their problems. And this idea is reinforced everywhere by our society. Americans spend billions of dollars every year on the diet industry. Dieting is such a common practice in the United States that many females believe it to be a rite of passage in life. But dieting has negative mental and physical consequences. Dieting means restricting the amount of food you eat. Your physical health suffers because your body doesn't get all the nutrients it needs. When losing weight is the ultimate goal, people begin to define themselves by a number on a scale. They can forget that there are many other qualities that define a person. Qualities such as intelligence, honesty, and a sense of humor are

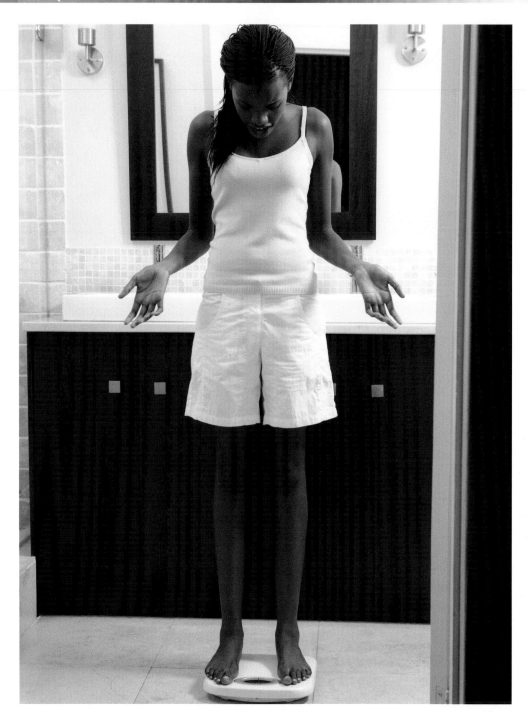

The number that appears when you step on a scale is only one part of the equation. Your weight doesn't factor in other important measurements, such as your height, muscle tone, and fat, not to mention your fitness level and overall health.

overshadowed by how much a person weighs and what a person looks like.

The body needs a certain amount of calories every day. The food we eat is converted into fuel for the body to carry on its normal functions. When we do not provide the body with this necessary fuel, it tries to conserve fuel by slowing down its rate of metabolism. Metabolism is the rate at which the body burns calories. When this rate is lowered, it means the body burns fewer calories and stores fat more efficiently.

When you eat less, your body responds by holding on to any food it gets. When a person goes off the diet, the body will regain all, if not more, of the weight lost during the diet. This is because the metabolism rate does not return to normal after a diet.

In addition to being ineffective, dieting also can physically damage the body—especially the body of a growing teenager. The teen years are a time of great mental and physical growth. During this time, the body is changing from a child's body into an adult's body. The body needs all the right nutrients to make this transformation successfully. When the body doesn't receive them, it will not be able to develop properly. Important bodily functions, such as a young woman's menstruation, may be delayed.

A lack of nutrients, such as calcium, can also lead to osteoporosis later in life. This disease causes a decrease in bone mass. The bones weaken and break easily. During the teen years, a lack of calcium can increase the risk of stress fractures. According to Dr. Susan Greenspan, director of the Osteoporosis Prevention and Treatment Program at the University of Pittsburgh Medical Center, studies indicate that nine out of ten teenage girls and seven out of ten teen boys do not get sufficient calcium in their daily diets. Many teens drink sodas instead of milk. Milk is a good source of calcium. Sodas actually leach calcium from bones.

Another danger of dieting is the attitude it can create. When a diet is unsuccessful, a person's self-esteem suffers. He or she may feel like a failure when weight is not lost permanently. He or she can begin an unhealthy cycle of yo-yo dieting. Yo-yo dieting is a term used to describe a cycle of beginning and quitting a diet several times. A person might focus all his or her attention on losing weight. He or she might begin to lose touch with reality and become desperate in the quest to lose weight. Taking diet pills or other weight-loss products is only the beginning of an unhealthy pattern of behavior. This pattern might eventually lead to the development of an eating disorder.

Taking It Too Far: Eating Disorders

Eating disorders include anorexia nervosa, bulimia nervosa, and binge eating disorder (compulsive eating). Compulsive exercise is also a growing problem and classified by experts as a related eating disorder problem. A person can have one or more of these disorders, and anyone can suffer from them—men and women of all ages and from all walks of life.

Anorexia Nervosa

The medical condition known as anorexia nervosa is usually shortened to anorexia. Although the word "anorexia" means "loss of appetite," the opposite is true. Those with anorexia are hungry all the time. Their weight is at least 15 percent below average for their height and age. They are starving themselves, sometimes to death. But those with anorexia fear putting on weight and often see themselves as heavier than they really are. Anorexia

Those who suffer from anorexia nervosa have a distorted body image and fear carrying excess weight. Anorexia is a severe psychological disorder that causes serious physical complications.

causes many physical problems. Because the body has so little fat, it can't maintain a normal body temperature. As a result, fine hairs, called lanugo, grow all over the body to try and keep it warm. People with anorexia are frequently cold, even in summer.

Young women with anorexia suffer from amenorrhea, which means that menstrual periods stop. Near-starvation and the resulting lack of calcium may cause osteoporosis later in life. Starvation also weakens the heart, which can develop a slow or irregular beat. Loss of fluids can cause dehydration. Dehydration can lead to an electrolyte imbalance in the body, causing death.

Anorexia also causes emotional problems. Because people who have anorexia tend to isolate themselves from family and friends, they might suffer from depression. Lack of food can harm the person's ability to think straight and concentrate. It can also cause a person to feel irritable, unhappy, and pessimistic most of the time. According to the National Association of Anorexia Nervosa and Associated Disorders (ANAD), 20 percent of anorexics will prematurely die from anorexia-related complications, including suicide and heart problems.

Bulimia Nervosa

Bulimia nervosa is characterized by binge and purge cycles. Bingeing is eating a large amount of food in a short amount of time. Purging is trying to rid the body of the food by vomiting, using laxatives to bring on a bowel movement, abusing diuretics to increase urination, and abusing drugs that induce vomiting. Some people exercise excessively to rid the body of the calories.

Bulimia nervosa, or bulimia, causes many health problems as well. These include dry skin and hair, brittle nails, or bleeding gums. The teeth develop cavities or ragged edges from stomach acids brought up by frequent vomiting. Vomiting also puts tremendous strain on the stomach and esophagus. When the lining of the esophagus breaks down, an ulcer develops. Purging gets rid of food before nutrients are absorbed. Without these nutrients, the body can suffer from malnutrition.

In addition, repeated use of laxatives can cause painful constipation (an inability to have bowel movements). Abusing diuretics can cause dehydration. Using ipecac syrup to induce vomiting is extremely dangerous and can cause congestive heart failure and death.

Bulimia can cause the same emotional problems that people with anorexia develop. Because people who suffer from bulimia keep their binge/purge cycles a secret, they can feel isolated and alone and suffer from depression. ANAD reported that 50 percent of those who suffer from anorexia develop bulimia. About one million of the eleven million people who suffer with anorexia and bulimia are male.

Binge Eating Disorder

Binge or compulsive eaters (sometimes called compulsive overeaters) are people who eat in response to psychological stress. In doing so, they eat when they're not hungry. Like those with bulimia, compulsive eaters go on food binges. Some compulsive eaters graze, eating many times during the day or night. People who compulsively overeat may wish to lose weight, but they do not purge food from their bodies.

Compulsive eating is psychologically damaging because people use food as a way to deal with uncomfortable feelings. Because they may not feel safe expressing sadness, anger, or other emotions, they eat as a way to find comfort. Also, most people with this disorder are overweight and may be at risk for other health problems, such as heart disease and diabetes. Being overweight alone does not always cause health problems, but it can be a problem when combined with an inactive lifestyle.

Binge eating is a characteristic of both bulimia nervosa and binge eating disorder. Binge eaters gorge on large quantities of food to feed an emotional, not a physical, hunger.

It's important to remember that the symptoms of these eating disorders can be interchangeable. Keep this in mind if you are concerned that you or someone you love has an eating disorder. Here are some general warning signs to watch for.

Do You Have an Eating Disorder?

Some common signs of eating disorders are:

- Constantly thinking about the size and shape of your body
- Constantly thinking about how much you weigh and repeatedly weighing yourself
- Constantly thinking about food, cooking, and eating
- Eating only certain foods in specific and limited amounts
- Wanting to eat alone and feeling uncomfortable eating with other people
- Not feeling good about yourself unless you are thin but never being satisfied with how thin you are
- Feeling that you should exercise more, no matter how much you already exercise
- Feeling competitive about dieting and wanting to be the thinnest or the smallest
- Keeping a list of what foods are OK to eat
- Taking diet pills or abusing laxatives and/or diuretics
- Continuing to diet, even after you are thin
- Purposely losing lots of weight very quickly
- Forcing yourself to throw up
- No longer having your monthly period

You'll notice that some of the above warning signs of an eating disorder are similar to the signs of a negative body image. This is because having a negative body image is closely linked and can lead to eating disorders. Negative body image is on a continuum, or a range, of severity. People who suffer from a negative body image are more likely to have an eating disorder as well. They usually go hand in hand. Keep in mind that you don't have to have every symptom on this list to suffer from a negative body image or to have an eating disorder. If some of these signs seem familiar to you, please consider speaking to a trusted adult and getting help.

Hurting Yourself: Self-Mutilation

It has many names: self-injury, self-injurious behavior, self-abuse, self-cutting, and repetitive self-harm syndrome. It is most often called self-mutilation. Regardless of what name you use, it is the

People who engage in cutting are known as self-mutilators. Self-injury can be appealing for someone who wants to feel physical pain to release tension, but it is not a healthy method of coping.

intentional destruction or alteration of one's own body tissue without conscious suicidal intent.

Self-mutilation includes many acts, such as cutting, skin carving, burning, scratching, bone breaking, picking scabbed wounds, and trichotillomania—repeatedly plucking out one's hair or eyelashes and eyebrows.

Most often, self-mutilators are female and are likely to suffer also from an eating disorder. There are many reasons why people cut, burn, or engage in other self-injurious acts. It can be a way to convert unbearable emotions into tolerable physical pain. Some people say they self-mutilate because they are emotionally numb and it helps them feel something. Others say it helps them express anger or release tension.

Self-mutilation, eating disorders, and a negative body image are very difficult issues. Those who suffer might not think it's right or normal to express feelings, such as anger or rejection. But feelings aren't right or wrong, they just are. Learning to cope with and express them is a big part of understanding who you are.

Getting Help

Eating disorders and self-mutilation are serious matters. They can permanently damage the body, and a person may need hospitalization. A person can also die from an eating disorder or self-mutilation. Even with professional help, the recovery process can be long and difficult, but many people do recover and go on to live successful, healthy lives. The sooner the disorder is diagnosed and treated, the better the recovery outcome will be.

If you think you might be suffering from one or more of these eating disorders, it's important that you reach out for help. Frequently, people who suffer from eating disorders do not acknowledge that they are ill. Talk to someone you trust, such as a coach, a guidance counselor, a teacher, or a family member and seek professional help. Only then can you begin to recover from the disorder and take back control of your life.

CHAPTER FOUR

Learning to Accept Your Body

Now that you know the signs of negative body image you can determine whether you have one. And now that you are aware of the dangers in having a negative body image, hopefully you are motivated to do something about it before it's too late.

However, overcoming negative body image isn't easy. You have built up certain habits and feelings for much of your life. It will take a lot of work and forgiveness, but you can find peace with your body. It may be the hardest thing you ever do, but it's also one of the most important things you'll ever do for yourself. Changing your body image is a process that you will have to work on for many years, if not the rest of your life. The most important thing to remember is that recovery comes through changing your attitude, not your body. Feeling good about yourself is the key to making healthy decisions about how to care for and celebrate your body.

Change can begin by simply educating yourself—reading books and contacting organizations that deal with the dangers of the beauty ideal, negative body image, and eating disorders. But if your problems are more serious, you will need to seek more help.

Treatment Through Counseling

Because having a negative body image is an indication of larger problems in your life, treatment must involve attacking the causes behind it. This can involve psychological counseling, which will help you deal with emotions in a healthy way. It's very important to learn how to handle stress, anger, and frustration without taking it out on your body. Both individual therapy and group therapy are positive ways to accomplish this goal. Contact organizations such as the National Association of Anorexia Nervosa and Associated Disorders (ANAD) or the National Eating Disorders Association (NEDA), which can direct you to more resources, or talk to a trusted adult or friend.

You might also benefit from a support group. There are many support groups around the country that offer a confidential and

Expressing your feelings to others who have similar struggles in the safety of support groups and group therapy is a valuable way to deal with negative body image.

comfortable atmosphere to discuss your problems with people who have similar feelings and experiences. If there isn't one in your area, you can start your own. See the For More Information section at the back of this resource for ideas on where to look in your area.

Learn About Nutrition

Having a negative body image often results in unhealthy eating patterns. Speaking with a registered dietitian or nutritionist at your school or family clinic about food and nutrition will help you understand why your body needs food, vitamins, and minerals to function properly. You'll also learn why your body needs fat in order to stay healthy. You'll learn that eating a variety of different foods is healthy and that eating in response to hunger rather than emotional needs will help you reach your goals.

A registered dietitian can help you relearn normal eating patterns. Nutritionist Ellyn Satter, author of *Child*

Learning about nutrition may help you understand the importance of what you put into your body. Food is not your enemy: its job is to fuel and nourish your body. A proper diet includes things you might believe are bad, such as fats and carbohydrates.

Exercise is essential for a healthy body and mind. But don't think of exercise as a means to keep weight off. Working out should be something you enjoy, so find an activity that's fun for you and enjoy the health benefits that accompany it.

of Mine: Feeding with Love and Good Sense (2000), writes, "Normal eating is flexible. It varies in response to your hunger, your schedule, your proximity to food, and your feelings. Normal eating takes up some of your time and attention, but keeps its place as only one important area of your life."

Focus on Your Health, Not the Scale

Having a negative body image often means a person spends most of his or her time focusing on weight. Part of finding peace with your body means changing your focus. Knowing a little bit about genetics can help you do that.

Everyone has his or her own individual set point of weight. This set point is the weight your body naturally falls to when you eat well and exercise regularly. It varies from person to person, much like hair color or eye color. This set point is determined mostly by your genetic makeup. This means that your body shape and size are established by the genes you inherited from your parents. You have only so much control over how much you weigh and what your body looks like.

In addition, many experts are starting to believe that overall health is more important than your weight. Your health depends more on how much you exercise and what kinds of foods you eat than on how much you weigh. In other words, it's not fat that matters, it's fitness and health.

It's important to exercise because it keeps your body healthy, not because it burns calories. Otherwise, you risk becoming obsessed with your exercise routine. Moderation is the key. The Centers for Disease Control and Prevention and the American Council on Sports Medicine recommend about half an hour of moderate exercise three or four days each week. But that doesn't mean you need to go

to extremes. Exercise should be fun and something you enjoy. The types of activities you do can vary, from riding a bike to gardening or even cleaning up your room!

This information can help you begin to accept your body shape and to appreciate yourself and other people for their unique qualities. Weight is not only something you have little control over, but you can be perfectly healthy if you eat right and get regular exercise—no matter how much you weigh. As you stop focusing on your weight and body shape, you can begin to spend time on more productive things in your life.

Throughout your recovery process, it can be helpful to write down your routines and feelings. Keeping a journal can teach you behavior patterns, and it can serve as a confidant for all your personal feelings. You might have good days and bad days, and you

Recording your eating and exercise habits, even for a short time, can reveal a lot about your lifestyle that you might be unaware of. This can also be a good emotional outlet.

will progress and regress. Writing down everything will help you get through the difficult times. Remember to treat yourself with kindness and forgiveness, and try to counter every negative thought you have with a positive one.

10 GREAT QUESIONS TO ASK A COUNSELOR

1. Is it normal that my weight fluctuates weekly and sometimes daily?

2. How can I learn to like exercise and to do it in a healthy way?

3. How do I know what size is healthy for me?

4. How can I learn to listen to my body when it tells me I am hungry or full?

5. Do I have an eating disorder, and if so, how long do you think the treatment process will be?

6. What can I do to love myself more?

7. How can I tell my friends I'm having problems with my body image?

8. How can I stop comparing myself to models and celebrities?

9. How long will it take me to improve?

10. Will these feelings go away when I get older?

CHAPTER FIVE

Change the Conversation

Instead of wondering why you don't measure up to the beauty ideal, why not flip the script? Why don't models and actresses look like you? There is an astounding lack of diversity in the media, despite changing attitudes. For instance, Dove's Campaign for Real Beauty attempts to use real women with varying body types as models to show that there is no one beauty ideal. Still, Dove's advertisements are in the minority. Most companies use young, stick-thin, light-skinned models to promote their products.

So what can you do about it? Many feel that fighting back against society's unrealistic ideals helps people change their own ideals. Speaking out and fighting back can provide a release for all those negative thoughts. Taking action can increase your self-confidence and give you a sense of purpose. There are people and organizations fighting against negative media messages. Join them in their efforts and you will begin to see results.

Employ Critical Thinking

One way to feel better about your body image is to become a critic. Think about the fact that advertising executives are trying to get you to buy their products. They want you to believe that if you buy their products, you will look just like the models in the advertisements. But you know that these ads are not representations of reality.

Instead of swallowing all that the beauty industry is trying to feed you, step back and think for a minute. Do they have your best interests at heart? What is their ultimate goal?

Every time you see an ad that starts to make you feel bad about your body, stop and think: What does this advertiser want me to think? (That the model is handsome or beautiful and I should look more like him or her.) What is this advertiser trying to get me to do? (Spend my money on the products in the ad.) Why would the advertiser want me to believe the beauty ideal is real? (So the advertiser can make millions of dollars!)

You Have Buying Power

Once you start to look at the beauty industry with a critical eye, you can begin to reject the beauty ideal as the big lie that it is. After all, how many real people do you know who look anything like the models we see in magazines and on television?

You are a valuable consumer to advertisers. They care about what you think because they want you to buy their products. If you see an advertisement, a movie, a music video, or anything else that

Beauty comes in all shapes, colors, sizes, and ages. Think about the times when you have felt happiest and most beautiful. Did you look like you stepped out of a magazine?

you don't like or that encourages the stereotype that thin is good and fat is bad, use your voice and speak out. In addition, if you see messages that promote positive and diverse images of men and women, write letters to those companies to tell them you support their efforts.

Be a Health Ambassador

Help your friends recognize that healthy bodies come in many shapes and sizes and express appreciation for diversity. Instead of vowing to each other that you'll never eat again, why not start your own positive body image/high self-esteem club? Get together and talk about all the great things you do that have nothing to do with how you look.

You can work on changing family attitudes, too. Don't participate in name-calling based on appearances. Compliment family members for their accomplishments (as well as their looks). Share information about the dangers of dieting and eating disorders. And encourage high self-esteem in your whole family by showing appreciation and love for all family members.

Focusing on nutrition instead of your weight, and on success instead of ways you don't measure up, are steps you can take toward leading a productive and happy life.

Creative Exercises That Really Work

It isn't easy to develop a positive body image. It takes time. But here are some exercises that can help you on your journey.

- Before you say negative things about your body, ask yourself if you would ever say these words to a friend or loved one. If you wouldn't say such mean things to others, why is it acceptable to say them to yourself? If you see a part of your body you don't like, think about why you feel it is unacceptable and who benefits from your thinking this way.

- Make a list of all the wonderful things your body makes possible every day—whether it's singing, walking, dancing, playing sports, or giving someone a hug.

- Change the critical voice inside your head that talks down to you. When you start to think negatively about yourself, stop and look at what you are thinking, ask yourself what triggered the feelings, and then challenge what you are saying to yourself. Take the time to repeat your good qualities to yourself every day.

- Write a letter to yourself talking about all your excellent abilities that have nothing to do with how you look. Don't be shy—read it out loud in front of the mirror! Or make a list of your best friend's top ten qualities that don't have anything to do with appearance, and ask him or her to do the same for you. Then mail them to each other.

One simple way of beginning to change your self-image is to look in the mirror every morning as you're getting ready and tell your reflection how amazing you are. Don't talk about your appearance; instead, list all your best qualities and accomplishments.

- Make a list of friends, family members, teachers, and other people whom you know and admire. Write down what it is besides their appearance that makes them so special. Aren't these people more inspiring role models than those you see in the fashion magazines?
- Set goals for yourself that have nothing to do with how you look. Get involved in different clubs or activities and explore your various interests. Write down all of your achievements—including both tiny and huge ones—and congratulate yourself for each one.
- Express yourself and all your creative qualities! Stop comparing yourself to others. Keep a journal, paint a picture, write stories, make a craft, play an instrument—whatever it takes to remind yourself that there is much, much more to you than how you look.

You might be surprised how these exercises can change the way you see yourself and others. If you go back to them regularly, you might even change the way you think. Remember, however, that if you suspect you are suffering from an eating disorder, depression, or another disorder, You should seek professional help. You cannot do it alone. Talk to your parents, a trusted teacher, or another adult. They will help guide you toward treatment. Your goal should be loving and accepting yourself and becoming the best person you can be.

ADOLESCENCE Preteen and teen years of a person's life when a person is changing from a child into an adult.

ANOREXIA NERVOSA An eating disorder whose sufferers drastically reduce calorie intake in order to lose weight.

BINGEING Eating a large amount of food in a short amount of time.

BULIMIA NERVOSA Eating disorder marked by periods of bingeing and purging.

CONTINUUM Range.

DEHYDRATION The process of losing water or bodily fluids.

DEPRESSION Feelings of sadness and hopelessness that last a long period of time.

EATING DISORDER An unhealthy and extreme concern with weight, body size, food, and eating habits.

ELECTROLYTE IMBALANCE A life-threatening condition in which a person doesn't have enough of the minerals the body needs to maintain healthy fluid balance.

ESOPHAGUS A muscular tube that connects the back of the mouth to the stomach.

GENETIC Influenced by genes, which we inherit from our parents and which determine physical traits.

MENSTRUATION Female monthly bleeding, sometimes called a period.

NUTRIENTS Vitamins, minerals, and other food ingredients that your body needs to stay healthy.

OBSESSION A persistent and disturbing preoccupation with an unhealthy or unreasonable idea or feeling.

OSTEOPOROSIS A disease that results in a decrease in bone mass.

PSYCHOLOGICAL Having to do with the mind.

PUBERTY The time when a person's body becomes sexually mature.

PURGING Ridding the body of food by vomiting, excessive exercise, or abusing laxatives or diuretics.

ROLE MODEL A person you can look up to and admire for who he or she is and the things he or she has done.

SELF-ESTEEM Confidence, self-respect, and satisfaction with oneself.

STEREOTYPE An oversimplified opinion based on general or limited information.

YO-YO DIETING A cycle of weight loss and weight gain.

About-Face
P.O. Box 191145
San Francisco, CA 94119
(415) 839-6779
Website: http://www.about-face.org
About-Face promotes positive self-esteem in girls and women
of all ages, sizes, races, and backgrounds through a spirited
approach to media education, outreach, and activism.

The Alliance for Eating Disorders Awareness
1649 Forum Place, #2
West Palm Beach, FL 33401
(866) 662-1235
Website: http://www.allianceforeatingdisorders.com
This organization seeks to establish easily accessible programs
across the nation that allow children and young adults the
opportunity to learn about eating disorders and the positive
effects of a healthy body image. It aims to disseminate
educational information to parents and caregivers about the
warning signs, dangers, and consequences of anorexia,
bulimia, and other related eating disorders.

Binge Eating Disorder Association (BEDA)
637 Emerson Place
Severna Park, MD 21146
(855) 855-BEDA (2332)
Website: http://bedaonline.com
BEDA promotes excellence in care for those who live with, and
those who treat, binge eating disorder and its associated
conditions. BEDA is committed to promoting cultural

acceptance of, and respect for, the natural diversity of sizes, as well as promoting a goal of improved health, which may or may not include weight change.

National Association to Advance Fat Acceptance (NAAFA)
P.O. Box 4662
Foster City, CA 94404-0662
(916) 558-6880
Website: http://www.naafaonline.org
Founded in 1969, the National Association to Advance Fat Acceptance (NAAFA) is a nonprofit human rights organization dedicated to improving the quality of life for fat people. NAAFA works to eliminate discrimination based on body size and provide fat people with the tools for self-empowerment through public education, advocacy, and member support.

National Association of Anorexia Nervosa and Associated Disorders, Inc. (ANAD)
750 E. Diehl Road, #127
Naperville, IL 60563
Helpline: (630) 577-1330
Website: http://www.anad.org
ANAD is a nonprofit corporation that helps people with eating disorders. It provides information about various eating disorders, including methods of treatments and their effectiveness, and offers information about support groups, how to find a support group located near you, and how to start a support group.

National Association for Males with Eating Disorders (NAMED)

164 Palm Drive, #2

Naples, FL 34112

Website: http://www.namedinc.org

NAMED is a nationwide professional association committed to
leadership in the field of male eating disorders. The organization aims to provide support for males affected by eating
disorders, provide access to collective expertise, and promote the development of effective clinical intervention and
research in this population.

National Eating Disorders Association (NEDA)

165 West 46th Street, Suite 402

New York, NY 10036

(800) 931-2237

Website: https://www.nationaleatingdisorders.org

NEDA works to prevent eating disorders and provides treatment referrals to people who have eating disorders and
body image and weight issues. NEDA also publishes and
distributes educational materials about prevention and
eating disorders and operates a hotline.

Websites

Because of the changing nature of Internet links, Rosen Publishing
has developed an online list of websites related to the subject of
this book. This site is updated regularly. Please use this link to
access this list:

http://www.rosenlinks.com/CED/Body

FOR FURTHER READING

Bellenir, Elizabeth. *Eating Disorders Information for Teens*. Detroit, MI: Omnigraphics, 2013.

Boyle, Caitlin. *Operation Beautiful for Best Friends*. New York, NY: Grosset & Dunlap, 2012.

Collins-Donnelly, Kate. *Banish Your Body Image Thief*. London, England: Jessica Kingsley Publishers, 2014.

Conway, Celeste. *Body Image and the Media*. Minneapolis, MN: ABDO Publishing, 2013.

Haerens, Margaret. *Eating Disorders*. Detroit, MI: Greenhaven Press, 2012.

Palser, Barb. *Selling Ourselves: Marketing Body Images*. North Mankato, MN: Compass Point Books, 2012.

Pipher, Mary. *Reviving Ophelia: Saving the Selves of Adolescent Girls*. New York, NY: Ballantine Books, 1995.

Rissman, Rebecca. *Asking Questions About Body Image in Advertising*. Mankato, MN: Cherry Lane Publishing, 2015.

Royston, Angela. *Skin Deep: The Business of Beauty*. New York, NY: Gareth Stevens Publishing, 2013.

Smith, Rita P. *Self-Image and Eating Disorders*. New York, NY: Rosen Publishing, 2013.

Smolin, Lori A., and Mary B. Grosvenor. *Nutrition and Eating Disorders*. New York, NY: Chelsea House Publishers, 2011.

Taylor, Julia V., and Melissa Atkins Wardy. *The Body Image Workbook for Teens*. Oakland, CA: Instant Help Books, 2014.

Warbrick, Caroline. *Talk About Eating Disorders and Body Image*. London, England: Wayland, 2012.

About the Authors

Viola Jones teaches middle school and writes books for young adults. She lives in the Hudson River Valley with her husband and daughters.

Edward Willett is an award-winning author of more than fifty books of fiction and nonfiction for children, adults, and young adults. He's previously written biographies of authors J.R.R. Tolkien and Orson Scott Card, as well as musicians Jimi Hendrix, Johnny Cash, and Janis Joplin. Willett is also a professional actor and singer. He lives in Regina, Saskatchewan, Canada, with his wife and daughter.

Photo Credits